Devotionals
for
WOMEN

52 Week Guide ̖̖̖ ̖̖̖ures,
reflections and pray̖ ̖ournal to
Overcome fear, anxiety, stress and
loneliness through God's love.

ADISAN Publishing AB

Denise Gilmore

Contents

This Journal Belongs To :

_____

_____

Introduction

There are many expectations for you as a woman in your life. Those expectations range from family and marriage expectations, to work expectations from your boss and colleagues, to friend peer pressure and even more worldly expectations for you. You can feel the fear and anxiety of whether or not you will be able to measure up at work, in school, and even at home with fitting in with your friends and family members. You can also feel the weight of loneliness in your heart when you haven't seen the people that you're used to seeing in quite a long time. As a woman you can also put unrealistic expectations on yourself when it comes to getting tasks done on time. You risk your emotional, physical, and mental well-being just to prove that you can accomplish those things to the people around you, and to prove it to yourself.

This book was created to inspire and encourage women of all ages to never give up in the face of their struggles, anxiety, or during periods of loneliness. You may be going through anxiety due to personal circumstances, or the pressures that this life brings upon you. You may also experience periods of loneliness due to family members being out of state, the business of life, and missing after work activities with friends. No matter your age, whether 20, 50 or 90, anxiety, fear and loneliness can strike at any time when you least expect it. So, it is important to have scriptures to cling to in order to combat Satan's attacks.

It is our hope that this 52-week devotional inspires women to conquer their fears, anxieties, stress and loneliness head on, with God's help. We hope that this devotional will help you gain insight on which scriptures to lean on during periods of anxiety, fear and loneliness in your life. We also hope that it will relieve some of the fears that you face daily, by reminding you that you are never fighting these battles alone. Remember, God is always with you, and He is never far away. We hope that this devotional inspires you and encourages you no matter what you may be facing in your life.

Get Rid of Anxiety

SCRIPTURE:

"Be anxious for nothing, but in everything by prayer and supplication, with thanksgiving, let your requests be made known to God; and the peace of God, which surpasses all understanding, will guard your hearts and minds through Christ Jesus."

PHILIPPIANS 4:6-7

ELUCIDATION:

Anxiety is something that can wreak havoc on your life, if you aren't careful. What are some things that you fear in life? Maybe you have fear of the future, or fear over your family's health, or uncertainty with your financial situation. Maybe you fear not being able to get ahead in your job. Another fear that you might have is whether your kids will succeed in school or college. You can even have anxiety about who they are hanging out with.

The good news that God has declared in our text that you don't have to be anxious about anything in your life. Instead of being anxious, pray about the things that are on your mind, with thanksgiving in your heart. Praying over your life instead of worrying about it, takes time and discipline. But once you make it a habit, it will help you to get closer to God.

Tell God what is on your heart. His peace will cover you like a warm blanket and fill your heart with peace that surpasses all human understanding. He wants to hear any and all of your concerns, no matter how big or small they may be. He longs to fill you with His peace.

REFLECTION:

What anxieties can you get rid of by turning them over to God every day? If you practice turning worry into prayer every day, it will become a habit of your life. It will help you focus on Him and help you rest assured in His promises.

PRAYER:

Lord, help me to turn over any worries about my life over to you. Please fill my heart with the peace that can only come from you. Help me to turn to you and talk to you about any fears that I have. Please guide me and guard my heart and mind in Christ Jesus.

❧ ❧
I'm grateful for:

_____
_____
_____
_____
_____
_____
_____
_____
_____
_____
_____
_____

❧ ❧
My Thoughts:

_____
_____
_____
_____
_____
_____
_____
_____
_____
_____
_____
_____

❧ ❧
Prayer Requests:

_____
_____
_____
_____
_____
_____
_____
_____
_____
_____
_____
_____

❧ ❧
Prayers Answered:

_____
_____
_____
_____
_____
_____
_____
_____
_____
_____
_____
_____

Comfort in God

SCRIPTURE:

*"The Lord will perfect that which concerns me; Your mercy,
O Lord, endures forever; Do not forsake the works of Your hands."*

PSALM 138:8

ELUCIDATION:

The Lord will help you in all of you endeavors. As a woman, you take on many things in your life. You take care of yourself, your family, and even take care of your friends. Whatever God has put before you, whether it's responsibilities at work, at home, or anywhere in between, God will help you accomplish the task that He has put in front of you. Even more than that, His word says He will perfect the work that concerns you.

When things aren't going your way in life, do you ever think that God isn't with you? Everyone has thought that at one time or another in their lives. It is perfectly ok to call upon God and ask Him to help you through the tasks that seem impossible. Don't lose heart no matter how difficult the task in front of you seems. God's mercies are with you and His mercies endure forever. Believe that His promises stand true and know that God will not forsake the work of His hands over your life.

REFLECTION:

*Do you take comfort in knowing that the Lord will perfect His ways over your life?
How amazing is it that His mercies will endure with you forever? Believe in His
promises that He will not forsake the works of His hands and that He will help
you complete each daily task. Believe that He will help you complete everything
to the best of your ability.*

PRAYER:

*Lord, please help me to remember that every task that I have to do
is a blessing from you. Help me to remember that your mercies are
perfect and that you will perfect whatever concerns me in my life.
Please do not forsake me in the works of your hands.
Thank you that you will help me accomplish each task,
no matter how daunting it may seem.*

I'm grateful for:

_____
_____
_____
_____
_____
_____
_____
_____
_____
_____
_____
_____
_____

My Thoughts:

_____
_____
_____
_____
_____
_____
_____
_____
_____
_____
_____
_____
_____

Prayer Requests:

_____
_____
_____
_____
_____
_____
_____
_____
_____
_____
_____
_____
_____
_____

Prayers Answered:

_____
_____
_____
_____
_____
_____
_____
_____
_____
_____
_____
_____
_____
_____

Trust God with Your Worry

SCRIPTURE:

"Trust in the Lord with all your heart, and lean not on your own understanding; In all your ways acknowledge Him, And He shall direct your paths."

PROVERBS 3:5-6

ELUCIDATION:

How much do you trust the Lord? Do you trust Him in small matters and big matters in your life? What does it truly mean to put your trust in the Lord and rely on the Lord fully? It means to trust Him no matter how good or bad things are in your life. It also means surrendering your ways, your thoughts and all your worries to Him on a daily basis. Daily surrender to God takes much discipline, time and patience. It is ok to ask God for help to remember how and when to submit to Him in both big and small aspects of your life.

When this passage says to lean not on your own understanding, it means look to Him for understanding and not think that you can do things well on your own. Fully submit your ways to God. When the Bible says do not lean on your own understanding, it means to not think that you know more than anyone else in life. In everything you do you can always acknowledge Him, and He will surely direct your path. When you put your trust in Him and rely on His guidance, your life's path will become easier to understand.

REFLECTION:

How comforting it is to know that God allows you to come to Him and to be able to trust Him fully. To know that you don't have to lean on your own understanding and that he already knows which path your life will take. All you have to do is trust Him and acknowledge Him in everything you do and He will show you which paths to take.

PRAYER:

Lord, please help me to submit my ways over to you. Your ways are so much better than mine. Help me to see that I don't have to have everything figured out, but that you will direct my paths. Please help me to trust you and to acknowledge you in everything I do.

I'm grateful for:

_____
_____
_____
_____
_____
_____
_____
_____
_____
_____
_____
_____

My Thoughts:

_____
_____
_____
_____
_____
_____
_____
_____
_____
_____
_____
_____

Prayer Requests:

_____
_____
_____
_____
_____
_____
_____
_____
_____
_____
_____
_____

Prayers Answered:

_____
_____
_____
_____
_____
_____
_____
_____
_____
_____
_____
_____

Take Away My Burdens

❧·❧

SCRIPTURE:

*"Cast your burden on the Lord, And He shall sustain you;
He shall never permit the righteous to be moved."*

PSALM 55:22

❧·❧

ELUCIDATION:

What does it mean to cast? It means to throw away. What then does it mean in this passage when it says "Cast your burdens on the Lord"? It means that you can give your anxiety over to God any time, no matter what you may be going through. Giving your burdens to the Lord takes discipline. So many times, you can end up asking and even telling the Lord to take away whatever is making you anxious, and try to put it into His hands for a while. Then Satan starts making you think about the burdens you placed in God's hands. Then you start worrying about them all over again. It is a vicious, never ending cycle and a daily battle that you must be prepared to fight.

Even in the midst of this battle, you can trust that He will take care of you. He will sustain you. He sees you as a righteous and precious gift. He will not give you more than you can handle. He will never cast you out of His sight, or allow you to be moved to a place where you can't put your worries in His hands. He is willing to take your burdens from you.

❧·❧

RESPONSE:

Are you ready to give up any and all your burdens to the Lord? How do you think you'll feel when you give them up to Him? Believe that He will take care of you and that He will sustain you, no matter the anxiety you may be experiencing.

❧·❧

PRAYER:

*Lord, please help me to turn any and all of my burdens over to you.
Whenever I feel anxiety creeping into my mind, remind me that
you are and that you will take care of me. Thank you for always
being here for me. Thank you for always giving me a way out of my
anxiety. Thank you that I can always turn to you for strength, love
and support. Thank you for taking my burdens off my shoulders.*

I'm grateful for:

_____

_____

_____

_____

_____

_____

_____

_____

_____

_____

_____

_____

_____

My Thoughts:

_____

_____

_____

_____

_____

_____

_____

_____

_____

_____

_____

_____

_____

Prayer Requests:

_____

_____

_____

_____

_____

_____

_____

_____

_____

_____

_____

_____

_____

Prayers Answered:

_____

_____

_____

_____

_____

_____

_____

_____

_____

_____

_____

_____

_____

You are not Alone

❧·❧

SCRIPTURE:

"Where can I go from Your Spirit? Or where can I flee from Your presence? If I ascend into heaven, you are there; If I make my bed in hell, behold you are there. If I take the wings of the morning, and dwell in the uttermost parts of the sea. Even there Your hand shall lead me, And Your right hand shall hold me."

PSALM 139:7-10

❧·❧

ELUCIDATION:

Have you ever felt as though you were so alone that God wasn't even with you anymore? If you've ever experienced that deep despair of loneliness, you are not the only one. Maybe you felt the loneliness of not being able to see family members or friends. Maybe you feel the pain of loneliness of not being able to conceive or adopt a child, while your friends were able to have kids or adopt.

The good news is that even though you may feel alone at times and even though you may feel abandoned by your friends, your family and even abandoned by God, He is always with you. There is absolutely no place that you could ever go to hide from God. In this passage it reminds you that no matter where you travel and no matter what you do or even what you feel, His hand will lead you in your life. You are never far from His grace and His helping hand.

❧·❧

RESPONSE:

What comfort can you find in this passage, knowing that you are never far away from God's helping hand? How amazing is it to know that no matter where you go or what you do, Jesus is right there alongside of you every step of the way? Even though you may feel alone, with God in your life, you're never ever alone.

❧·❧

PRAYER:

Lord, thank you for revealing to me that I'm never really alone. Thank you for reminding me that you are always with me. Help me to remember that you are leading me in the way that you want my life to go.

❧ ❧
I'm grateful for:

_____
_____
_____
_____
_____
_____
_____
_____
_____
_____
_____
_____
_____
_____

❧ ❧
My Thoughts:

_____
_____
_____
_____
_____
_____
_____
_____
_____
_____
_____
_____
_____
_____

❧ ❧
Prayer Requests:

_____
_____
_____
_____
_____
_____
_____
_____
_____
_____
_____
_____
_____

❧ ❧
Prayers Answered:

_____
_____
_____
_____
_____
_____
_____
_____
_____
_____
_____
_____
_____

Negative Thoughts About Myself

SCRIPTURE:

*"I will praise You, for I am fearfully and wonderfully made;
Marvelous are Your works, and that my soul knows very well."*

PSALM 139:14

ELUCIDATION:

Have you ever thought negative thoughts about yourself? Have you ever thought that you weren't made for any special reason? You don't have to fear who you are or what you are going to become in your life. You don't have to compare yourself to other people. Just because they might be doing their lives at a faster pace than you, they already have a job, or a house, doesn't mean you are any worse than they are. You also don't have to think so negatively of yourself because God made you perfect just the way you are.

You're going about your life in the exact time, and at the exact pace that God wants you to be at. You have unique and awesome abilities that no one else has. You have a purpose in your life from the Lord Himself. You are special to Him and precious in His sight. This passage reminds you that you are fearfully and wonderfully made. God's work in your life is marvelous. Take the time to look back at how He has come through for you in the past and trust that He will come through for you again in your future.

REFLECTION:

What negative thoughts have plagued your mind recently? What negative thoughts have you said out loud about yourself in the past? Instead of comparing yourself to others, remind yourself that you are God's child. Remember that God's work in your life is marvelous. You are fearfully and wonderfully made and have a divine purpose!

PRAYER:

Lord, please help me to remember that comparison is the thief of joy in my life. Help me not to compare myself or beat myself up when things may not be going as quickly as I'd like. Help me to rest in the comfort that your works in my life are wonderful and that everything in my life will happen with your guiding hand at the right time. Help me to trust you.

I'm grateful for:

_____
_____
_____
_____
_____
_____
_____
_____
_____
_____
_____
_____
_____

My Thoughts:

_____
_____
_____
_____
_____
_____
_____
_____
_____
_____
_____

Prayer Requests:

_____
_____
_____
_____
_____
_____
_____
_____
_____
_____
_____
_____
_____

Prayers Answered:

_____
_____
_____
_____
_____
_____
_____
_____
_____
_____
_____
_____

God Hears You

❦

SCRIPTURE:

"For we wrestle not against flesh and blood, but against principalities, against powers, against the rulers of the darkness of this world, against spiritual wickedness in high places."

EPHESIANS 6:12

❦

ELUCIDATION:

The fight against anxiety, fear, and loneliness is a daily battle of will, courage and determination. It is also a battle to turn to God no matter how you may be feeling. This passage talks about how your fight is not against flesh and blood but against Satan and the darkness of sin in this world.

It is also a battle to turn to God and remember that you are fighting not just a physical, mental and emotional battle each day. You are also fighting a spiritual battle each day. Satan will attack your spirit and try to make you think less about God, and more about your problems. Every day you can make the choice to turn away from Satan and his darkness and turn all of your fears and anxieties and your feelings of loneliness over to God. Knowing that you are fighting a spiritual battle is the most important reminder to trust God and turn to Him instead of giving into the negative thoughts that Satan puts in your head. Tune into God's word and realize the power it brings you. Fight off Satan with positive affirmations about who you are in Christ.

❦

REFLECTION:

What peace and clarity can this scripture bring to you? Does it bring you comfort knowing that even though you're fighting against Satan and his dark schemes, God has given you the ability to resist Satan? He has given you the ability to turn to Jesus to fight against your stress, anxiety, fear and loneliness.

❦

PRAYER:

Lord please remind me that even though there are forces against me emotionally and mentally and even spiritually in this world, that you are still with me through all of it. Help me to fight against Satan every day by remembering the promises in Your Word. Give me the clarity and the courage to resist Satan and his schemes. Help me to remember who I am in Christ!

✦ ✦
I'm grateful for:

_____
_____
_____
_____
_____
_____
_____
_____
_____
_____
_____
_____
_____

✦ ✦
My Thoughts:

_____
_____
_____
_____
_____
_____
_____
_____
_____
_____
_____
_____
_____

✦ ✦
Prayer Requests:

_____
_____
_____
_____
_____
_____
_____
_____
_____
_____
_____
_____
_____

✦ ✦
Prayers Answered:

_____
_____
_____
_____
_____
_____
_____
_____
_____
_____
_____
_____
_____

Positivity through Strength

SCRIPTURE:

"I can do all things through Christ which strengthens me."

PHILIPPIANS 4:13

ELUCIDATION:

Instead of saying things like "I can't do this,", "this is too hard. I'll never accomplish this task correctly", start declaring positivity over your life every day. Start realizing the power you have within you from God Himself and start telling yourself these things each day, especially when things start getting difficult. "I am qualified for whatever task God puts in front of me". "I am able to handle whatever obstacles that come my way". "I have unique, God given abilities that no one can ever take away from me." "I have strength from God within me. I have God's power residing in me." "No matter the obstacles in my path or the odds stacked against me, I can and will do all things to the best of my ability with God's help!" "No matter how lonely I may feel, I know God is always with me and His power rests within me!"

 Don't doubt yourself, speak the words of Jesus over yourself. Speak life over yourself. Speak victory over your life in Jesus name. There is nothing you can't do with Christ at your side. Use this scripture to speak the truth from God over your life. Start believing that you actually are able to do anything and everything through Christ Jesus.

REFLECTION:

How often do you believe that you can do all things through Christ who gives you strength? What things will you be able to accomplish when you put this scripture into practice? You are able to do amazing things once you start believing in the abilities that God has given you.

PRAYER:

Lord, no matter how things are going in my life, please help me to remember that I can accomplish many amazing things with the strength that you give me. Help give me clarity to resist the Devil's schemes. Help me to speak the truth of Your Word over my life, instead of giving into stress, anxiety, fear or thoughts of loneliness.

I'm grateful for:

_____
_____
_____
_____
_____
_____
_____
_____
_____
_____
_____
_____
_____

My Thoughts:

_____
_____
_____
_____
_____
_____
_____
_____
_____
_____
_____
_____
_____

Prayer Requests:

_____
_____
_____
_____
_____
_____
_____
_____
_____
_____
_____
_____
_____

Prayers Answered:

_____
_____
_____
_____
_____
_____
_____
_____
_____
_____
_____
_____
_____

God has Plans for Your Life

✤•✤

SCRIPTURE:

*"For I know the thoughts that I think toward you,
saith the Lord, thoughts of peace, and not of evil,
to give you an expected end."*

JEREMIAH 29:11

✤•✤

ELUCIDATION:

God knows the plans He has for you in your life. No matter what may be going on, it can bring you immense comfort to know that God has a plan for your life. His plans are always better than your plans. He wants to bring you peace, hope and a future.

He doesn't want you to suffer with debilitating anxiety attacks or to lose sleep worrying about things in your life. Even when you are filled with worry about your life, trust that His plans are good and that He will bring you a great future. Trust that He knows what will happen before anything even happens. Let it bring you comfort that He wants things to go well for you in your life. He wants to see you smile and enjoy life to the fullest extent. He doesn't like seeing you suffer. He will help you look forward to each day. All you have to do is seek Him with all your heart.

✤•✤

REFLECTION:

Do you have hope about your future? Since God knows the plans He has for your life, you can rest assured that He is for you, not against you. He wants to help you in your life, and He wants you to have hope and not work yourself to the bone. Don't forget to take the time to rest in His goodness as you walk towards your future. Give your plans over to God and watch Him work in marvelous ways that you never thought possible!

✤•✤

PRAYER:

Lord, please help me to remember the plans that you have for my life are much better than my own, whenever I get overwhelmed. Help me to focus on your plan and the hope that you have for me in my life instead of giving into the worry that can plague my mind. Help me to rest in the assurance that you want me to have peace in my life.

※·※
I'm grateful for:

_____
_____
_____
_____
_____
_____
_____
_____
_____
_____
_____

※·※
My Thoughts:

_____
_____
_____
_____
_____
_____
_____
_____
_____
_____
_____

※·※
Prayer Requests:

_____
_____
_____
_____
_____
_____
_____
_____
_____
_____
_____
_____
_____

※·※
Prayers Answered:

_____
_____
_____
_____
_____
_____
_____
_____
_____
_____
_____
_____
_____

Spiral of Toxic Thoughts

✤•✤

SCRIPTURE:

"For my thoughts are not your thoughts,
neither are your ways my ways, saith the Lord."

ISAIAH 55:8-9

✤•✤

ELUCIDATION:

God knows you even more than you know yourself. He knows your thoughts before you even speak them or think them. If you think too much about your stress and your fears, you can start to think negatively about yourself. The next time you start having an anxiety attack or panic attack, remind yourself that those thoughts that are plaguing you, are from Satan and not from God. Remind yourself that your thoughts toward yourself aren't God's thoughts towards you. God only thinks good thoughts toward you.

Whenever you think your life should go a certain way in your life, remember that God's ways are not your ways. Remind yourself that even though it may be tempting to try to get things to go your own way, God's ways are always better than your ways. He can do more for you in your life than you could ever do for yourself. He can and will do amazing things in your life that can only come from knowing Him personally as your Lord and Savior!

✤•✤

REFLECTION:

Have you ever suffered anxiety attacks because you let your thoughts wander too much? How can you ask God to help you counter act any thoughts that make you anxious? Trust that His ways are infinitely better than your ways. Take captive the thoughts that God thinks of you, not what you think of yourself. Start speaking God's affirmations over your mind, body, and your life.

✤•✤

PRAYER:

Lord please protect my mind from the thoughts of the enemy.
Help me to think good thoughts about my life and to trust that
you are helping keep my mind at peace. Help me to remember
that your ways are always better than mine. Thank you for always
bringing peace to my thoughts, and for thinking wonderful
thoughts about me. Thank you for your love!

I'm grateful for:

_____
_____
_____
_____
_____
_____
_____
_____
_____
_____
_____
_____
_____

My Thoughts:

_____
_____
_____
_____
_____
_____
_____
_____
_____
_____
_____
_____
_____

Prayer Requests:

_____
_____
_____
_____
_____
_____
_____
_____
_____
_____
_____
_____

Prayers Answered:

_____
_____
_____
_____
_____
_____
_____
_____
_____
_____
_____
_____

I think of my Lord

❧·❧
SCRIPTURE:

*"When thou liest down, thou shalt not be afraid:
yea, thou shalt lie down, and thy sleep shall be sweet."*

PROVERBS 3:24

❧·❧
ELUCIDATION:

Have you ever had sleep problems and insomnia due to anxiety? Have you ever woken up in the middle of the night freaked out by the possibilities of all the things that could go wrong in your life? What triggers your anxiety and your fears? Sometimes your anxiety can get out of control. Once you take the time to figure out the triggers of your anxiety, you can do your best to eliminate them.

No matter the anxieties in your life, there is hope in God's word. Through this passage, He wants you to lie down and sleep in peace. He also wants you to have a restful night's sleep so you can continue to do the work He has laid out for you. You don't have to be afraid of the way things will go in your life. He doesn't want you to be afraid. Praying for peace can often calm your mind very quickly and help you fall back asleep. Rest in His promises that He will protect you and guide you in your life.

❧·❧
REFLECTION:

*What things and scenarios are you afraid of in your life? What racing thoughts keep
you from getting the restful and peaceful night's sleep that you deserve? Ask God
through prayer to calm your racing mind each night and to give you a peaceful night's
sleep. Trust in Him that your sleep will be sweet.*

❧·❧
PRAYER:

*Lord, please help my mind to stay on you. Help calm my anxiety
and fears, so that I can sleep well each night. Help me to rest assured
in your promise that if I trust in you, my sleep will be sweet every
night. Thank you that you can and will help me overcome my fears.*

꙰

I'm grateful for:

_____

_____

_____

_____

_____

_____

_____

_____

_____

_____

_____

_____

_____

꙰

My Thoughts:

_____

_____

_____

_____

_____

_____

_____

_____

_____

_____

_____

_____

_____

꙰

Prayer Requests:

_____

_____

_____

_____

_____

_____

_____

_____

_____

_____

_____

_____

_____

꙰

Prayers Answered:

_____

_____

_____

_____

_____

_____

_____

_____

_____

_____

_____

_____

_____

Gift of God

SCRIPTURE:

"Then Mary said, "Behold the maidservant of the Lord! Let it be to me according to your word." And the angel departed from her."

LUKE 1:38

ELUCIDATION:

Have you ever received startling news out of the blue from someone in your life? Maybe you got news from your doctor about a diagnosis that you weren't expecting, or a friend or family member tells you that a loved one has unexpectedly passed away. Your first reaction would no doubt be utter shock which would then give way to sadness. Have you ever received good news from people in your life about a job promotion, or that you no longer have an illness that you've been fighting? What important tasks have you been given in your life?

Can you imagine the way Mary must have felt when the angel Gabriel visited her and told her that she would have Jesus without ever being intimate with a man before? She was told that she would give birth by the power of the Holy Spirit! No doubt that Mary was in shock and awe too. But after the initial shock wore off, she accepted what the angel said to her by saying "let it be done unto me according to your word." She accepted the task that the Lord had given her with courage, strength, and dignity. We too, can accept the tasks that God has given us with the same courage, strength and dignity that Mary had.

REFLECTION:

What tasks have you been given by God in your life? Have you changed your attitude about the tasks that you've been given from "why me?" to, "let it be done unto me according to your word"? If you graciously accept the tasks that God has placed in your life, God will bless the works of your hands.

PRAYER:

Lord, please help me to accept the tasks that you've placed in front of me. Help me to see each task as a gift from you. Help me to see each task as important and to take the responsibility for each task willingly, just as Mary did.

_____
_____
_____
_____
_____
_____
_____
_____
_____
_____
_____
_____
_____

❧·❧

Prayer Requests:

❧·❧

Prayers Answered:

_____
_____
_____
_____
_____
_____
_____
_____
_____
_____
_____
_____
_____
_____

Fear of the Unknown

SCRIPTURE:

"For this child I prayed, and the Lord has granted me my petition which I asked of Him."

1 SAMUEL 1:27

ELUCIDATION:

What was your reaction when you found out that you were pregnant for the first time? Did you react with awe struck wonder, or were you filled with anxiety? Many women pray for the ability to conceive a child. While a lot of women are able to conceive naturally by God's grace, others have to go through invitro or adopt, or choose a surrogate to have a child.

Having a child is a big responsibility. Your whole life changes when you have a child. God making you a mother is one of His biggest blessings. It is also normal to feel anxiety and fear over the changes that your body is going through. It is also normal to fear going to the ultrasound appointments to see how your baby is developing. There is also that fear of the unknown about whether your child is developing properly. There is the uncertainty of how long you will carry the child and how your delivery will go. Everyone prays for a smooth delivery for both mother and child but sometimes that is not the case. Even though you may be filled with uncertainty, you can rest assured that God has His loving hands upon you and your child, from the day of conception, to their birth, and all throughout your child's life. Your pregnancy is a true blessing from God.

REFLECTION:

What things were you fearful of when you found out you were pregnant? How did God calm your fears about all the unknowns that are associated with pregnancy? Did you start to feel joy about having a child when you prayed that things would work out?

PRAYER:

Lord, I thank you for this child inside me. Thank you for allowing me to be able to have a child through adoption or through a surrogate if I choose to have a child that way. Thank you for blessing our family with this child. Help us to show him or her how to walk with you every day of their life.

I'm grateful for:

_____
_____
_____
_____
_____
_____
_____
_____
_____
_____
_____
_____
_____

My Thoughts:

_____
_____
_____
_____
_____
_____
_____
_____
_____
_____
_____
_____
_____

Prayer Requests:

_____
_____
_____
_____
_____
_____
_____
_____
_____
_____
_____
_____
_____

Prayers Answered:

_____
_____
_____
_____
_____
_____
_____
_____
_____
_____
_____
_____

You are God's Child

SCRIPTURE:

"But the very hairs of your head are all numbered. Do not fear therefore; you are of more value than many sparrows."

LUKE 12:7

ELUCIDATION:

Have you ever thought that things would keep going wrong in your life once they started spiraling out of control? Take this scripture to heart that God knows you, your heart and that He even knows how many hairs you have on your head. He even tells you that you are more valuable than sparrows. Since God knows how many hairs are on your head, you don't have to fear anything in your life. Even though things may be difficult at times, remember you are more valuable than the birds of the air.

God knows all the hairs on your head and even knows what number the hairs on your head are. If He knows those intricate details of your life, He will no doubt take care of you in every area of your life. Trust that He will work out things in His time and in His way and will bless your life.

REFLECTION:

What are you worried about in your life? Remember that God knows all of the intricate details of your life including every detail of the hairs on your head. He doesn't want you to fear about your life, whether there are big things or small things going on. Remember you are far more valuable than many sparrows.

PRAYER:

Lord, please help me not to worry about my life. Thank you that you know the intricate details of my life already, even down to the details about my body and the hairs on my head. Thank you for making me your child. Thank you for reminding me that I am even more valuable to you than many sparrows.

I'm grateful for:

_____
_____
_____
_____
_____
_____
_____
_____
_____
_____
_____
_____

My Thoughts:

_____
_____
_____
_____
_____
_____
_____
_____
_____
_____
_____
_____

Prayer Requests:

_____
_____
_____
_____
_____
_____
_____
_____
_____
_____
_____
_____

Prayers Answered:

_____
_____
_____
_____
_____
_____
_____
_____
_____
_____
_____
_____

Stop Worrying Start Praying

❦·❦

Scripture:

"You will show me the path of life; In Your presence is fullness of joy; At Your right hand are pleasures forevermore."

Psalm 16:11

❦·❦

Elucidation:

When you have kids, you tend to worry about them. That worry unfortunately only grows as they get older, become teenagers and then go off to college. When your kids go to college, you no doubt worry about their safety. But have you ever felt that sense of emptiness? Have you ever had that empty nest feeling?

Even though you may feel alone because your kids are no longer in your house anymore, you can learn to enjoy the time you now have to yourself. Even though you may fear the influences that may prey upon them in college, you can still trust that God will keep them safe. God will show them the path of life that He wants them to take. You can take comfort in knowing that God will guide them in all of their ways.

You can also take comfort in knowing that God will guide you through the new season of having an empty nest. You can be full of joy knowing that your kids get to experience the world with God at their side.

❦·❦

Reflection:

When your kids go off to college, what is the first thing you think about? Do you worry about the influences that they will have in their lives? Do you worry about their safety? What about the feelings that come over you with now having an empty nest? Even in the midst of that uncertainty, you can rest assured that God is with your kids and you as you navigate different seasons of your life. You will be filled with joy as you watch them navigate their way through life.

❦·❦

Prayer:

Lord, please be with my kids in every area of their lives. Please keep them safe in your care and let them experience the joy that comes from knowing you. Please help me learn to navigate having an empty nest and let me look forward to when my kids come home.

I'm grateful for:

_____
_____
_____
_____
_____
_____
_____
_____
_____
_____
_____
_____
_____

My Thoughts:

_____
_____
_____
_____
_____
_____
_____
_____
_____
_____
_____
_____
_____

Prayer Requests:

_____
_____
_____
_____
_____
_____
_____
_____
_____
_____
_____
_____
_____

Prayers Answered:

_____
_____
_____
_____
_____
_____
_____
_____
_____
_____
_____
_____
_____

Fear about Money, Food and Shelter

SCRIPTURE:

*"And my God shall supply all your need according
to His riches in glory by Christ Jesus."*

ROMAN'S 15:13

ELUCIDATION:

Have you ever worried about how you were going to make ends meet, or how you were going to pay for food for your family? Have you ever wondered where you next meal would come from? Everyone has fears about where the money will come from and asks themselves how they will pay for things in their life. You aren't the only one. The good news is that God promises you in His word that He will supply all of your needs by the grace of God.

No matter the need you may be facing, there is nothing that God can't provide for you. He knows your needs and the needs of your family before the words and prayers even come out of your mouth. God will provide the exact person, thing or circumstance in your life at the right moment, to help you make ends meet. He knows you need to keep heat on and a roof over your head. He also knows how to keep those blessings in your life. He will help you in ways that you never expected. He is always faithful.

REFLECTION:

*Have you ever spent too much time worrying about how you were going to pay for
your child's education, or how you were going to keep the heat on in the house? Those
are valid worries that you can have. But remember, the next time you feel strapped for
money or resources, God will often come to your rescue in the most unexpected ways.
He can and will come through in ways that you know can only be works of His hand.*

PRAYER:

*Lord, please help me to trust that you will help me through any
situation that may be causing me worry. Please bring the right person,
circumstance or payment into my life at your exact right moment.
Thank you that you've never failed me and that you never will.*

Prayer Requests:

Prayers Answered:

Trust God's Compassion

SCRIPTURE:

"Praise be to the God and Father of our Lord Jesus Christ, the Father of compassion and the God of all comfort, 4 who comforts us in all our troubles, so that we can comfort those in any trouble with the comfort we ourselves receive from God."

2 CORINTHIANS 1:3-4

ELUCIDATION:

God is the Father of all compassion. He is also the God of all comfort. Whenever you feel anxious, lonely or fearful, remember that you can always turn to God for peace and comfort. God comforts you in the midst of all your troubles so that you can lean on Him and rest in His assurance.

Through any trials you face, with God's help, you will be able to comfort other people who may be going through some of the same trials that you're going through. It truly is an honor to be able to go through trials, gain wisdom, and then pass on the valuable lessons you've learned from those trials, and be able to help someone else. It takes discipline to be able to see trials that you go through as learning experiences. To look beyond what you're going through and realize that your trial might actually point someone else to Christ, is such a special moment. Praise Him for the power to help someone else in the most difficult moments of their life.

REFLECTION:

How amazing it is to know that you can always turn to God for comfort in any trial? Have you ever been able to help someone else by telling them what you learned through a trial? Have you been able to give them the same comfort that God has given you? Cling to God for wisdom, discernment and comfort during your trials and He will give you wisdom to navigate through life.

PRAYER:

Lord thank you for being my comfort in times of trouble. Thank you for giving me comfort so I can take what you've taught me and go comfort someone else whenever they go through a hard time in their life. Thank you for helping me see each trial as a learning experience.

I'm grateful for:

_____
_____
_____
_____
_____
_____
_____
_____
_____
_____
_____
_____
_____

My Thoughts:

_____
_____
_____
_____
_____
_____
_____
_____
_____
_____
_____
_____
_____

Prayer Requests:

_____
_____
_____
_____
_____
_____
_____
_____
_____
_____
_____
_____
_____

Prayers Answered:

_____
_____
_____
_____
_____
_____
_____
_____
_____
_____
_____
_____
_____

God Saves Us

✦

SCRIPTURE:

"Who then is the one who condemns? No one. Christ Jesus who died—more than that, who was raised to life—is at the right hand of God and is also interceding for us."

ROMANS 8:34

✦

ELUCIDATION:

What is your favorite part of Easter? Is it spending time with your loved ones, watching your kids hunt for Easter eggs and meet the Easter Bunny? Or is it remembering the promise that God made to all of us that in 3 days Jesus would rise again from the dead and declare victory over sin, death and the power of the Devil? It is important to remind yourself and your family and to teach your kids that Jesus rising from the dead is the most important part of Easter. Don't be afraid to tell them about the Good News of Jesus and how His love saved us.

It is also important to remind yourself, your kids and your family that even though you go through hard times in your life, that Jesus is always interceding for you. This passage reminds you that Jesus really takes the time to talk to God on your behalf and wants you to remember that He is the true reason you celebrate Easter every year. There is nothing better than to gather with your friends and family and talk about the miracle of Easter.

✦

REFLECTION:

What is your favorite part of Easter? Remember that Jesus rose to life again on the third day and that He sits in Heaven by His Father's right hand, ready to interceded for you on your behalf. No matter what worries, fears or anxieties you have, Jesus is interceding to the Father on your behalf. You are never alone.

✦

PRAYER:

Lord, thank you that you great love for me allowed you to go to the cross to die for me. Thank you for forgiving my sins. Thank you for always interceding to God on my behalf. Please help me to remember to focus on you on Easter and every day.

I'm grateful for:

_____
_____
_____
_____
_____
_____
_____
_____
_____
_____
_____
_____
_____

My Thoughts:

_____
_____
_____
_____
_____
_____
_____
_____
_____
_____
_____
_____
_____

Prayer Requests:

_____
_____
_____
_____
_____
_____
_____
_____
_____
_____
_____
_____

Prayers Answered:

_____
_____
_____
_____
_____
_____
_____
_____
_____
_____
_____
_____

Shower Your Love

SCRIPTURE:

"Now therefore ye are no more strangers and foreigners, but fellow citizens with the saints, and of the household of God;"

EPHESIANS 2:19

ELUCIDATION:

What is your favorite memory of Thanksgiving? Is it eating all the food, spending time with your family, or enjoying time off from work? Some people don't get to spend Thanksgiving with their families. They might be in a nursing home, in the hospital, or alone at home because no one comes to visit them on holidays.

Those people may get easily overwhelmed by being alone on holidays. The important thing to do is to remind them that they aren't alone. You can do nice things for them such as sending them cards, or cooking them a nice Thanksgiving meal. You can also remind them that they are no longer stranger or foreigners, rather they are fellow citizens with the saints and the household of God. You can take the time during Thanksgiving to minister to them and to let them know you are thinking of them. Thanksgiving is one of the best times to share the good news of being a part of God's kingdom. Sharing that Good News with people who are struggling with loneliness in their life is an honor.

REFLECTION:

Have you ever felt alone during a holiday? Have you ever had your family say that they couldn't come to celebrate Thanksgiving with you? It probably made you feel disheartened didn't it? You can help other people who may feel alone on Thanksgiving by being there for them, reminding them that they are loved by God and that they are never alone.

PRAYER:

Lord please help me to remember how important it is to show your love to those who feel as though they are alone. Help take away their feelings of loneliness. During this wonderful Thanksgiving season, please help me to remind people of the Good News. Please give me the right words to remind them that they have a citizenship with you in Heaven. Thank you for your wonderful gift of life. Help me to be grateful for you not just on Thanksgiving but every day.

I'm grateful for:

My Thoughts:

Prayer Requests:

Prayers Answered:

Comparison is Thief of Joy

SCRIPTURE:

*"She is clothed with strength and dignity;
she can laugh at the days to come."*

PROVERBS 31:25

ELUCIDATION:

Have you ever felt as though you weren't good enough? Have you ever felt as though you couldn't meet someone's standards of you? Have you ever compared yourself to someone else? What about feeling as though you weren't special or feeling like you didn't have a purpose?

The good news is that you don't have to be hard on yourself like that. You are a daughter of the Most-High King. While you're feeling down about yourself, God wants you to remember that you are clothed in both strength and dignity. God also wants you to remember that He wants you to experience joy in your life. He doesn't want you to wallow in your self- pity and feel sorry about the way your life is going. He doesn't want you to think you aren't good enough or special enough. He doesn't want you to compare yourself to anyone else. No! He wants you to remember that you are His child! You are good enough! He wants you to be able to laugh at the days to come, and to enjoy every day of your life. Claim your strength and dignity with the power of the Holy Spirit!

REFLECTION:

Have you ever felt down about your life? Have you ever thought that someone always has it better than you? Do you compare your story to someone else's? Remember that you are a child of God, and He has a unique and awesome plan for you. Remember that God wants you to start acting like you are clothed in both strength and dignity and to be able to laugh at the days to come.

PRAYER:

Lord, please help me not to compare myself to anyone else. Help me to remember that you want me to enjoy life to its fullest and to laugh a lot in life. Whenever I start being hard on myself please remind me that I am clothed with your strength and dignity. Thank you that I am your child and that I'm treasured by you.

I'm grateful for:

_____
_____
_____
_____
_____
_____
_____
_____
_____
_____
_____
_____

My Thoughts:

_____
_____
_____
_____
_____
_____
_____
_____
_____
_____
_____
_____

Prayer Requests:

_____
_____
_____
_____
_____
_____
_____
_____
_____
_____
_____
_____

Prayers Answered:

_____
_____
_____
_____
_____
_____
_____
_____
_____
_____
_____
_____

Position of High Power

❧ · ❧

SCRIPTURE:

*"...and who knoweth whether thou art come
to the kingdom for such a time as this?"*

ESTHER 4:14

❧ · ❧

ELUCIDATION:

Do you remember the story of Queen Esther? She was a peasant girl who was chosen to be queen. Little did she know that God had placed her in that position of power for a very specific and special reason. She was to deliver her family and her people, the Jews from being put to death by King Xerxes and his right- hand man Haman. Esther was nervous and didn't think she was qualified to be Queen or that she was qualified to save her people. She almost backed out of telling the King about Haman's evil plot. Luckily, God gave her the courage to save herself and her people.

Have you ever felt as though you weren't qualified enough for a position or a task like Esther did? Maybe, you were put on earth for such a time as this to be in a position at work or at home, to do what God is calling you to do. Instead of being fearful that no one will listen to you, be brave like Esther and claim your position in the name of God. Do what He is calling you to do with courage!

❧ · ❧

REFLECTION:

Have you ever been put in a position of power that you didn't feel you were qualified to have? Maybe Gods is calling you to a position of higher power to help you show God's goodness to those around you. God has equipped you, called you and qualified you to whatever position you have, just as He called, equipped and qualified Queen Esther to save her people. Maybe you were put on Earth for such a time as this.

❧ · ❧

PRAYER:

Lord, please help me to be brave like Queen Esther for whatever calling you have placed in my heart and in my life. Help me to remember that you have placed me on Earth for such a time as this.

I'm grateful for:

_____
_____
_____
_____
_____
_____
_____
_____
_____
_____
_____
_____

My Thoughts:

_____
_____
_____
_____
_____
_____
_____
_____
_____
_____
_____
_____

Prayer Requests:

_____
_____
_____
_____
_____
_____
_____
_____
_____
_____
_____
_____

Prayers Answered:

_____
_____
_____
_____
_____
_____
_____
_____
_____
_____
_____
_____

Count My Blessings

❦·❦

SCRIPTURE:

"In the multitude of my thoughts within me thy comforts delight my soul."

PSALM 94:19

❦·❦

ELUCIDATION:

What do you do when you have an anxiety attack? Do you like to be around people or like to be by yourself? Some people feel more comfortable around their family or friends, while others like to be alone until the anxiety passes. How often do you go into God's presence or think good Godly thoughts during anxiety? Sometimes, you can get easily overwhelmed by the things that are going on in your life. Satan also likes to attack your mind. As a woman, you are often pulled into many different directions every day, as a wife, mom, worker, home-maker and an errand runner. Everything demands your attention and it can get very overwhelming.

The good news is that even though at times your thoughts can make you feel overwhelmed, God's helper, the Holy Spirit can bring you joy and cause you to rest in God's peace. It is ok to call out to God when you feel overwhelmed. In fact, He invites you to come to Him no matter how you may be feeling. Even in the midst of your anxious thoughts, go into His presence. Let His comfort bring delight to your soul.

❦·❦

REFLECTION:

What do you do in the midst of anxiety? Do you feel better after you call out to God in the secret of your own heart or out loud? When you take the time to rest your mind by allowing God to give you comfort, you will be able to get rid of the anxiety that might be in your heart. Take the time every day to think of the blessings that you have instead of the fears that you have about the future. Remember, you can control your thoughts every day with God's help.

❦·❦

PRAYER:

Lord please help me to remember to rest in your goodness whenever my thoughts start giving me anxiety. Please help me to think good thoughts any time I feel anxiety or fear. Help me to remember that your comfort can and will delight my soul.

❦

I'm grateful for:

_____
_____
_____
_____
_____
_____
_____
_____
_____
_____
_____
_____
_____

❦

My Thoughts:

_____
_____
_____
_____
_____
_____
_____
_____
_____
_____
_____
_____
_____

❦

Prayer Requests:

_____
_____
_____
_____
_____
_____
_____
_____
_____
_____
_____
_____
_____
_____

❦

Prayers Answered:

_____
_____
_____
_____
_____
_____
_____
_____
_____
_____
_____
_____
_____
_____

Rely on God

❧·❦

SCRIPTURE:

"For God hath not given us the spirit of fear;
but of power, and of love, and of a sound mind."

2 TIMOTHY 1:7

❧·❦

ELUCIDATION:

Fear is a normal feeling to go through. Everyone feels fear at one time or another. As a mother, you most likely feel fear and apprehension each time your kids leave the house, whether it's to go play at a friend's house, to drive to the store, or when they go off to college. At work and at home, you feel the stress of daily tasks weighing on your shoulders. You also worry about achieving statuses with your coworkers and bosses and what you can do to get them to like you more. You also worry about the health and safety of your family.

The good news that this Bile verse reminds you is that God didn't even give you a spirit of fear. The fear that you get is from Satan. He is trying to mess with your mind and your life. Thankfully God gave you the power within you to resist the devil and his schemes. God gave you a spirit of power, of love and a sound mind. With these tools you can resist Satan each time he tries to attack you or attack your family.

❧·❦

REFLECTION:

Do you give into the fear that Satan puts in your mind about your family, your work schedule, your ability to get every task done at home? God wants you to remember that He gave you a sound mind so that you can accomplish all the tasks in front of you to the best of your ability. He also gave you the ability to show love to everyone around you. You also have the power of self-discipline to know when you should and shouldn't speak.

❧·❦

PRAYER:

Lord please help me to remember the power that you have given me. Help me to learn to rely on you more instead of my own power. Help me to show love to everyone around me and to practice self-control whenever I think I need to speak out about something. Help my mind to stay steadfast on you.

I'm grateful for:

My Thoughts:

Prayer Requests:

Prayers Answered:

God's Comfort During Difficult Times

SCRIPTURE:

*"Yea, though I walk through the valley of the shadow of death,
I will fear no evil: for thou art with me;
thy rod and thy staff they comfort me."*

PSALM 23:4

ELUCIDATION:

Think about the toughest time you've gone through in your life. Was it the birth of your children? A family member dying? A friend suddenly walking out of your life? You may have felt as though your life was over at that time and you may not have been sure how you could go on living. You may have even felt as though you were walking through the valley of the shadow of death.

The valley of the shadow of death is a very scary place to be, physically, mentally, emotionally, and especially spiritually. Even though there will be times when you will feel as though you can't go on in your life, take comfort in this scripture. Even though you walk through the valley of the shadow of death, you do not have to fear the evil that may be around you, because God is with you at all times. God's rod and staff will bring comfort to you even in the midst of your hardest struggle.

REFLECTION:

What was it like for you going through the valley of the shadow of death in your life? Was there ever a time when you told God that you couldn't go on? Whenever the toughest time comes along, remember that you do not have to be afraid because God will remind you that He is always with you. Remember, even though you may not see it or feel it right away, the hardest times often will lead you to beautiful outcomes.

PRAYER:

Lord, whenever the hardest time comes in my life, please be with me. Help me to remember to rest in your comfort. Remind me that even though I can't see through the other side right now, that you will get me to the other side by your power and in your time. Thank you that I will get through this difficult time.

I'm grateful for:

_____
_____
_____
_____
_____
_____
_____
_____
_____
_____
_____
_____
_____
_____

My Thoughts:

_____
_____
_____
_____
_____
_____
_____
_____
_____
_____
_____
_____
_____
_____

Prayer Requests:

_____
_____
_____
_____
_____
_____
_____
_____
_____
_____
_____
_____
_____
_____

Prayers Answered:

_____
_____
_____
_____
_____
_____
_____
_____
_____
_____
_____
_____
_____

Feeling Overwhelmed

SCRIPTURE:

"Come unto me, all ye that labor and are heavy laden, and I will give you rest. Take my yoke upon you, and learn of me; for I am meek and lowly in heart: and ye shall find rest unto your souls."

MATHEW: 11:28-29

ELUCIDATION:

When was the last time you've felt overwhelmed? Everyone has felt overwhelmed at one time or another in their life. God is so good. He actually invites you to come to Him whenever you feel burdened from your daily work. He invites you into His calming presence to rest your mind, body and soul. You can learn from God how to rest yourself in His presence. Just being in His presence will fill you with a peace that you can't fully understand. God is gentle and humble in heart. He doesn't like seeing you suffer in fear, anxiety or loneliness in your life. Call upon Him and He will give you rest for your soul in more ways than one. He will literally take the anxieties off of your shoulders and put them on Himself. He will carry them for you, willingly.

REFLECTION:

Are you feeling overwhelmed right now? There is not a person on this earth who hasn't felt the same way. What are you overwhelmed about? Turn your worries over to God and He will give you rest from them. He will also teach you how to not worry as much in this earthly life. Remind yourself to turn to God whenever you feel as though you need a break in life. Don't be afraid to ask God to take away your burdens, or to ask Him for His to navigate your way through them. He will fill you with His peace.

PRAYER:

Lord, please help me to remember that I can come to you with any and all of my worries about this life. Help me to go into your presence whenever my soul needs a refresher. Thank you that I can go into your word and into your presence whenever I need to. Thank you for taking every burden that I'm feeling upon yourself on the cross.

I'm grateful for:

My Thoughts:

Prayer Requests:

Prayers Answered:

A True Friend

SCRIPTURE:

"God is our refuge and strength, an ever-present help in trouble."

PSALM 46:1

ELUCIDATION:

No matter what you may be going through in your life, whether it is anxiety, loneliness or fear, it is important to remember that even though thoughts can wander, God is your refuge and strength. Call out to Him in the midst of your loneliness and ask Him to bring your family around. Ask Him to bring a true friend into your life. Ask Him to calm whatever is making you upset. He is your ever-present help in times of trouble.

How often do you think to call on Him when you get stuck between a rock and a hard place? Most of the time, turning to Him for clarity and comfort is the last thing any of us remember to do. Rather, we tend to wallow in our worry and fret about things that aren't going our way for hours and even days at a time. Then all of a sudden, it dawns on us that we can turn to God for help through our problems. When we turn our problems and worries over to God, we are taking our focus off the problem and refocusing on the One who can and will fix the problem. Rely on Him for the strength that you didn't even know you had inside you.

REFLECTION:

What do you need God's help getting through in your life? Remember that you can turn your worries over to Him at any time, day or night. When you shift your focus off of the problem, and focus on the One who can fix the problem, it helps you remember that God is your ever-present help during difficult times.

PRAYER:

Lord please help me to remember to turn to you when things are difficult in my life. Please help me to remember that focusing on you will help me get through any troubles a lot faster. Thank you that I can call on you whenever I need to. Thank you for being my refuge and my ever-present help no matter what I may be going through.

I'm grateful for:

My Thoughts:

Prayer Requests:

Prayers Answered:

Self Blaming

*"A man that hath friends must shew himself friendly:
and there is a friend that sticketh closer than a brother."*

PROVERBS 18:24

ELUCIDATION:

If you have ever had friends walk out of your life unexpectedly, and suddenly asked yourself and God, "why did they leave my life?", you now the pain of uncertainty. Asking yourself why they left your life so suddenly will often mess with your mind and at times even your physical well-being. You might end up torturing yourself mentally going over what you could have done wrong to make them walk away. You might blame yourself for the friendship ending. It might give you anxiety wondering why friends walked out of your life.

But God could be protecting you from keeping bad company in your life. God knows who belongs in your life and who doesn't. It even says in this verse that one who has corrupt friends may come to ruin. However, there is a friend in our lives that will stick closer than a brother. His name is Jesus. He will never leave our lives unexpectedly. He is always with us, in spirit and wants us to know that He is always there for us. He is our truest and dearest friend.

REFLECTION:

Have you ever had a friend or a family member walk out of your life unexpectedly? Remember that there is a true friend in your life that will never abandon you or leave you. Does this promise in scripture bring you comfort that no matter who leaves your life, that Jesus is always in your life? Jesus will never leave you high and dry in your life. He wants to be close to you and have a great relationship with you. Remember, a relationship with a friend on Earth can't even compare to a relationship with Jesus!

PRAYER:

Lord, please help me to not blame myself when friends walk in and out of my life. Help me to remember that you know best about who belongs in my life and who doesn't. Thank you that I can always turn to you, as my best and truest friend.

❧•❧
I'm grateful for:

_____
_____
_____
_____
_____
_____
_____
_____
_____
_____
_____

❧•❧
My Thoughts:

_____
_____
_____
_____
_____
_____
_____
_____
_____
_____
_____

❧•❧
Prayer Requests:

_____
_____
_____
_____
_____
_____
_____
_____
_____
_____
_____
_____

❧•❧
Prayers Answered:

_____
_____
_____
_____
_____
_____
_____
_____
_____
_____
_____
_____

Persevere through Trials

SCRIPTURE:

"And not only so, but we glory in tribulations also: knowing that tribulation worketh patience and patience, experience; and experience, hope and hope maketh not ashamed; because the love of God is shed abroad in our hearts by the Holy Ghost which is given unto us."

ROMAN'S 5:3-5

ELUCIDATION:

Even though it might sound crazy to try to find glory or in other words, gladness in your sufferings, all your sufferings are meant to bring you closer to God. Even though you will struggle with stress, anxiety, fear and loneliness in your life, you know that you will find glory in the middle of your tribulations. Even though your tribulations will be difficult, those tribulations produce patience within your heart, mind and soul. They will produce patience within yourself and with those around you. Whether it's coworkers, family or friends. It will teach you to hold your tongue when you want to spout off in anger.

Patience produces perseverance in the midst of your trials. With patience you will be able to think more clearly and rationally. That will help you navigate your way out of a problem quicker and at times, much easier. Perseverance produces experience and character. Experience produces a much wiser character within you to navigate through the troubles that come your way. Character produces the hope that you cling to in Jesus. The hope you cling to in Jesus gives you the strength to persevere through any trials that come your way. You don't ever need to feel ashamed for knowing that Jesus gave you hope in the midst of your trials. Let God's love change you from the inside out.

REFLECTION:

How do your trials build your character? Do you feel proud of yourself when you persevere through trials? You don't have to be ashamed of going through trials. God's love is poured into your heart. Embrace trials because they show you how good God is.

PRAYER:

Lord please help me to persevere through trials. Thank you that you are with me even through the trials that seem too difficult to overcome. Remind me not be ashamed of the trials I go through.

✤·✤
I'm grateful for:

_____

_____

_____

_____

_____

_____

_____

_____

_____

_____

_____

_____

_____

✤·✤
My Thoughts:

_____

_____

_____

_____

_____

_____

_____

_____

_____

_____

_____

_____

_____

✤·✤
Prayer Requests:

_____

_____

_____

_____

_____

_____

_____

_____

_____

_____

_____

_____

_____

✤·✤
Prayers Answered:

_____

_____

_____

_____

_____

_____

_____

_____

_____

_____

_____

_____

_____

Purpose of My Life

✦

SCRIPTURE:

"And we know that in all things God works for the good of those who love him, who have been called according to his purpose."

ROMAN'S 8:28

✦

ELUCIDATION:

Even though you will have days with anxiety, don't beat yourself up over it. Don't think that you may never beat the anxiety. Every time you have anxiety, you can remember that God works for the good of those who love Him and those that are called according to His purpose. You have a personal relationship with God and you love Him. You want to get to know Him. You are called according to His purpose. He works all things together for your good because He loves you and you love Him. If you stay true to yourself and cling to His promises, you will see His goodness in your life.

Take the time to step back and think about what God has called you to do in your life. What is His purpose in your life? What is His purpose for your life? Take time to talk to Him and ask Him to fill you with His purpose for your life.

✦

REFLECTION:

Even though there will be days that you struggle, God will work things out for your good. Remind yourself that God has everything under control. You are called according to His purpose in your life. Ask God to reveal Himself and His ways to you. Don't be afraid to ask Him what His goals and His purpose is for you in your life. His purpose for your life, may just surprise you in marvelous ways!

✦

PRAYER:

Lord please help me to remember that through your power, ways and wisdom, everything in my life will work together for my good. Please remind me to not give up hope in the midst of my struggles. Thank you for having a purpose for me in my life. Help me to look for your purpose in my life rather than my own purpose. Thank you for always being with me. Reveal to me your plans and purpose for my life.

❦

I'm grateful for:

_____
_____
_____
_____
_____
_____
_____
_____
_____
_____
_____
_____
_____

❦

My Thoughts:

_____
_____
_____
_____
_____
_____
_____
_____
_____
_____
_____
_____

❦

Prayer Requests:

_____
_____
_____
_____
_____
_____
_____
_____
_____
_____
_____
_____

❦

Prayers Answered:

_____
_____
_____
_____
_____
_____
_____
_____
_____
_____
_____

Way out of Temptation

❦ SCRIPTURE:

"There hath no temptation taken you but such as is common to man: but God is faithful, who will not suffer you to be tempted above that ye are able; but will with the temptation also make a way to escape, that ye may be able to bear it."

1 CORINTHIANS 10:13

❦ ELUCIDATION:

When you are tempted to give into the sorrow of anxiety, you can remember that the temptation that you're going through, is the same as everyone else's temptation. As this scripture says, God is faithful and He will not let you be tempted to give into any fear or stress that you cannot bear. Whenever you feel yourself tempted to go into the pit of despair from the anxiety, remember that the anxiety is not permanent. It will pass. Whenever an anxiety attack comes on remember that God also gives you a way to escape it.

Ask God to help you figure out different ways to overcome the anxiety that comes into your life. You can and will overcome it in more ways than one. Read His Word to bring yourself comfort. Pray through the anxiety attack, asking God to calm your spirit. Read a good book. Memorize and say your favorite scriptures out loud whenever you feel anxious. Start declaring the blessings in your life instead of the stressors in your life. Give yourself time away from your tasks until the attack passes if you can. You can and you will overcome your anxiety physically, spiritually as well as mentally and emotionally.

❦ REFLECTION:

When you are tempted to give into the overwhelming feeling of anxiety, remember that God always gives you a way out of that temptation. You will overcome the anxiety with God's help. With prayer, you can feel God's peace wash over you and remind yourself that it won't last.

❦ PRAYER:

Lord, please help me to remember that I can get out of stress and anxiety at any time with your help. Help me to not give in to the sorrow of anxiety for too long, but rather help me to come to you when I have anxiety.

I'm grateful for:

_____
_____
_____
_____
_____
_____
_____
_____
_____
_____
_____
_____

My Thoughts:

_____
_____
_____
_____
_____
_____
_____
_____
_____
_____
_____
_____

Prayer Requests:

_____
_____
_____
_____
_____
_____
_____
_____
_____
_____
_____
_____
_____

Prayers Answered:

_____
_____
_____
_____
_____
_____
_____
_____
_____
_____
_____
_____
_____

God fights My Battles

Scripture:

"The Lord shall fight for you, and ye shall hold your peace."

Exodus 14:14

Elucidation:

When you're overwhelmed with stress, fear, loneliness or anxiety in your life, you can take comfort in the fact that God will fight for you in every battle that you face. All you have to do is be still and tell Him whatever is on your mind. Tell Him what you're feeling. Tell Him why you're struggling with your fear, anxiety, or loneliness.

Ask Him to take away the anxiety and to fill your heart with the peace that can only come from Him. Ask Him to calm your spirit in ways that only He can. Ask Him to take your loneliness away by putting true friends in your life. Remind yourself that you can leave all of your anxiety in God's hand and rest in peace.

Reflection:

Ask God to fight your battles for you and He will give you His peace in your heart. Ask Him to bring the correct people into your life to help you overcome your anxiety, fear and loneliness. Ask Him to bring the right tools into your life to beat your anxiety. By praying and reading His word, you will get through your anxiety and loneliness day by day.

Prayer:

Lord please help me to rest in the assurance that you are fighting my battles. Each day help me to not get overwhelmed but to give you all of the daily battles I deal with. Thank you for fighting my battles for me.

I'm grateful for:

_____
_____
_____
_____
_____
_____
_____
_____
_____
_____
_____

My Thoughts:

_____
_____
_____
_____
_____
_____
_____
_____
_____
_____
_____

Prayer Requests:

_____
_____
_____
_____
_____
_____
_____
_____
_____
_____
_____

Prayers Answered:

_____
_____
_____
_____
_____
_____
_____
_____
_____
_____
_____

God's Restoration Power

SCRIPTURE:

*"But may the God of all grace, who called us to His eternal glory
by Christ Jesus, after you have suffered a while, perfect,
establish, strengthen, and settle you."*

I PETER 5:10

ELUCIDATION:

What things do you struggle with on a daily basis? Maybe you stress about getting tasks done at home or at work. Maybe you are overwhelmed with trying to help your kids excel in their schooling. Maybe you are being hard on yourself because you haven't figured a way out of your anxiety. Maybe you long to have lasting friendships in your life. Have you ever doubted that God was really there for you?

Isn't it comforting to know that even though you will deal with anxiety, fears, loneliness and other trials in this world, God Himself will restore you and make you strong again? That means that after you have struggled for a while, He will help you. He will also establish you with the correct people in your life at the right time. He will also establish you with the right tools to do the tasks that you are assigned to do. He will strengthen you and help you through your anxiety each day and with His peace He will settle your anxious mind.

REFLECTION:

Remember all of the times that God brought you through your anxiety, friendship struggles, your loneliness and your fears. Whenever you start doubting, remember how He has brought you through trials and that He will do it again.

PRAYER:

*Lord, please let me never lose sight of you in the midst of my
struggles. Please help me to remember that you've gotten me
through my friendship struggles, my anxiety and my feelings of
loneliness and that you will do it again. Help me to trust that
you will put the right people in my path at the right time. Please
establish me on the correct path in school, at work and at home.
Settle my mind and help me to rest in your love. Thank you for
always giving me a way through my struggles.*

❧ ❧
I'm grateful for:

_____
_____
_____
_____
_____
_____
_____
_____
_____
_____
_____
_____
_____

❧ ❧
My Thoughts:

_____
_____
_____
_____
_____
_____
_____
_____
_____
_____
_____
_____
_____

❧ ❧
Prayer Requests:

_____
_____
_____
_____
_____
_____
_____
_____
_____
_____
_____

❧ ❧
Prayers Answered:

_____
_____
_____
_____
_____
_____
_____
_____
_____
_____

God never Abandoned Me

SCRIPTURE:

"I will not leave you orphans; I will come to you."

JOHN 14:18

ELUCIDATION:

God has promised you that He will not leave you as an orphan in your life. Instead He will adopt you into His family by giving you the free gift of salvation and by believing in Christ Jesus. Once you are in God's family, you can rest assured that you will never be left alone ever again. God will come to you and give you peace, rest, love, joy, and most of all, unconditional love.

You are never alone when you have a relationship with Christ. That relationship with Him is the most important relationship you could ever have in your life. It gives you someone to turn to in the midst of your struggles, and it gives you someone to talk to about your fears. The more you get to know Him the more you'll want to know about Him. Even though there will be times that you will feel alone in life, you are never alone and you are never far away from God. He will show His power in your life. Trust in His promise that He will never leave you as an orphan. You are adopted into God's eternal family and have eternal life waiting for you in heaven.

REFLECTION:

Doesn't it bring you comfort to know that you are never left alone or abandoned by God? Get to know Him every day by reading His word and by doing daily devotions. You can even join a weekly Bible study with people in your church and your friends. You can also get to know Him by talking to Him in daily prayer. Ask Him to reveal things to you about what it means to be His Child and you will be surprised at what He teaches you throughout your life.

PRAYER:

Lord, please open my eyes to your goodness. Help me to want to learn more about you every day. Thank you that you adopted me into your eternal family by salvation in Your Son Jesus.

❦

I'm grateful for:

_____
_____
_____
_____
_____
_____
_____
_____
_____
_____
_____
_____
_____
_____

❦

My Thoughts:

_____
_____
_____
_____
_____
_____
_____
_____
_____
_____
_____
_____
_____
_____

❦

Prayer Requests:

_____
_____
_____
_____
_____
_____
_____
_____
_____
_____
_____
_____
_____

❦

Prayers Answered:

_____
_____
_____
_____
_____
_____
_____
_____
_____
_____
_____

Most Important thing in Life

❖·❖

SCRIPTURE:

"Charm is deceitful and beauty is passing,
But a woman who fears the Lord, she shall be praised."

PROVERBS 31:30

❖·❖

ELUCIDATION:

As a woman, you carry many hats in your life. What is the most important thing that you do in your life? You do many tasks in your daily life and you try to live up to the expectations of others and the expectations that you set for yourself. You try to sound intelligent in front of your co-workers, your boss and your family and friends. You put on makeup to make yourself look more beautiful. You dress up when you go out to important occasions. You also try to be charming whenever you go out on dates. Those things aren't important compared to being a woman who knows Jesus as her personal Lord and Savior.

As it says in the verse, charm is deceitful, and beauty is something that will pass quickly. But a woman who fears the Lord and knows the Lord will be praised. Knowing Jesus is the most important thing you can ever do in your life. It is more important than money, status, makeup, relationships, friendships, or even your family. Having a relationship with Him can and will change your life. Knowing Jesus is also the most important value that you can teach your children, your husband and everyone else in your life.

❖·❖

REFLECTION:

Have you reevaluated what the most important thing in your life is? There is nothing more important than having a relationship with Jesus and helping others in your life get to know Him. Money, work status, possessions and all other Earthly things don't matter. As long as you keep Jesus at the center of your life, everything else in your life will fall into place.

❖·❖

PRAYER:

Lord, please help me know you. Let my thoughts of you be the first thing on my mind in the morning and the last thing on my mind before I go to sleep. Thank you for teaching me throughout my life that you are the only thing that matters. Help me to be an example of your love in everything I say and do.

I'm grateful for:

_____
_____
_____
_____
_____
_____
_____
_____
_____
_____
_____
_____
_____

My Thoughts:

_____
_____
_____
_____
_____
_____
_____
_____
_____
_____
_____
_____
_____

Prayer Requests:

_____
_____
_____
_____
_____
_____
_____
_____
_____
_____
_____
_____
_____

Prayers Answered:

_____
_____
_____
_____
_____
_____
_____
_____
_____
_____
_____
_____
_____

Daily Chores

SCRIPTURE:

"God is in the midst of her, she shall not be moved;
God shall help her, just at the break of dawn."

PSALM 46:5

ELUCIDATION:

If you ever feel overwhelmed by the tasks that you have to do every day, remember that you have God's strength within you. When you have a relationship with God you actually have the spirit of God inside of you. He will guide you on which paths to take, when to speak out and when to not speak out.

He also helps you lead others to Christ by helping you tell people in your life the Good News. He guides you every single moment of your life. No matter what trials you go through, even though you will fail at times, every failure is a learning experience. Even through your failures, God is still with you and He wants to help you. You will not be moved, as long as you remain steadfast in your faith.

God will help you from the moment you wake up and start your day to the time when you go to sleep at night. He will help you accomplish every task that you have in front of you, whether you have tasks at work, school or at home. Keep your eyes on Him at all times. He knows you will fail at times and turn away from Him, but He is always there to redirect your path. He is always there to help you every step of the way.

REFLECTION:

Isn't it comforting to know that God will help you in every step that you take throughout your day? As long as you keep your eyes on Him each day, you will feel His presence. He knows you are trying your best. He always offers His help to you in every situation.

PRAYER:

Lord, please help me to keep my eyes fixed on you through my entire day. Help me to remember that I can rely on you through anything that comes my way. Thank you that your spirit is within me. Thank you that I can always turn to you for help in any situation.

I'm grateful for:

_____
_____
_____
_____
_____
_____
_____
_____
_____
_____
_____

My Thoughts:

_____
_____
_____
_____
_____
_____
_____
_____
_____
_____
_____

Prayer Requests:

_____
_____
_____
_____
_____
_____
_____
_____
_____
_____
_____

Prayers Answered:

_____
_____
_____
_____
_____
_____
_____
_____
_____
_____
_____

Serve My People

❦·❧

SCRIPTURE:

*"She extends her hand to the poor,
Yes, she reaches out her hands to the needy.
She is not afraid of snow for her household,
For all her household is clothed with scarlet."*

PROVERBS 31:20-21

❦·❧

ELUCIDATION:

Think of all the people who don't have enough food, water, or a place to live within your community. Have you ever been in a position where you were wondering what you wondered where your next meal or drink was coming from? Have you ever been in a position to help the needy within your community? If you give what you have to the poor, and help the needy, God will see your humble attitude and will reward you. Helping others who are less fortunate can help you realize how blessed you are.

Even though it can be nerve-wracking to help people you don't know, when you help others you feel amazing don't you? When you bless others around you, especially those that you don't know, God will bless you. You don't have to be afraid of any difficulty that might come over you and your family because you are protected by God. Even though Satan might put fear into your heart, don't be afraid to step outside your comfort zone and to help others.

❦·❧

REFLECTION:

When was the last time you served people in your community or in your neighborhood? How did it make you feel? Did you see people's needs and realize just how blessed you were in life? Realizing how good you have it in life, puts more room in your heart to serve others.

❦·❧

PRAYER:

Lord, please help me to realize how blessed I am in my life. Everything that I have is a gift from you. Thank you for allowing me to have the ability to serve others. Thank you for showing me what it means to serve other people in my community. Help me to not be afraid to serve others that I don't know.

I'm grateful for:

My Thoughts:

Prayer Requests:

Prayers Answered:

Stay Calm in every Situation

❧•❧

SCRIPTURE:

"Likewise, their wives must be reverent, not slanderers,
temperate, faithful in all things."

I TIMOTHY 3:11

❧•❧

ELUCIDATION:

This verse means that as a woman and a wife, you are to be treated with respect at all times. You are also supposed to treat others with respect. That means even though you may be going through anxiety, or struggling with loneliness, you still have to try to remain calm in every situation. Even though you may be fighting fears of many different kinds, you have to remind yourself to stay calm. Even though there will be days where you will fight anxiety, this verse reminds you that anxiety doesn't give you the right to talk bad about someone else or to show anger towards others.

When you treat others with respect, they will treat you with respect. Being calm in every situation will help you figure things out faster, and put you in a better frame of mind. Being trustworthy when someone tells you something in private, means not telling anyone else what the person just told you. When you honor someone by keeping what they said to you private, you are also honoring God by being kind to that person. You are also honoring god by keeping what the person said private.

❧•❧

REFLECTION:

Is it ever hard to remain calm when you have anxiety? If you have ever felt that way you
aren't alone. When you are trustworthy with your friends and family members doesn't
it make you feel good that you can talk openly to them and they can talk to you about
anything? Doesn't it feel better to remain calm instead of being anxious in every situation?
You can train your mind to stay calm and turn to God for guidance in every situation.

❧•❧

PRAYER:

Lord please help me to remember to stay calm in every situation.
Please help me to remember to treat everyone with respect. Thank
you for the opportunity to be trustworthy to people.

I'm grateful for:

My Thoughts:

Prayer Requests:

Prayers Answered:

These tough times will pass

❦

SCRIPTURE:

"Fear not, O land; Be glad and rejoice,
For the Lord has done marvelous things!"

JOEL 2:21

❦

ELUCIDATION:

Even though there are many things to fear in your life, such as fear of the way things are going in your life, anxiety over your family's wellbeing, God tells you that you don't have to fear. Rather, you can be glad and rejoice that God has given you many great blessings in your life.

Take a minute to think of the blessings that you have in your life. You have your family, your job, your friends, your relationship with God, your unique abilities are all blessings. Even though you will go through difficult times in your life you can rejoice because those times will teach you lessons that you will never forget. Be grateful for the blessings you have.

Those tough times will pass. Once they pass you will remember what you learned and will be able to rejoice again. The Lord has promised that He will do great things in your life. All you need to do is trust that He will do the things He said He would do. Even when you can't see Him, He is always working behind the scenes of your life.

❦

REFLECTION:

Have tough times ever made you forget the Lord's promises? Rather than wallowing in self-pity, remind yourself that God has come through for you during hard times in the past and that He will do it again.

❦

PRAYER:

Lord please help me to focus on you during hard times. Help me to remember that you have been with me before and that you will deliver me from hard times again. Thank you that you are doing marvelous things in my life.

❦

I'm grateful for:

_____
_____
_____
_____
_____
_____
_____
_____
_____
_____
_____
_____
_____

❦

My Thoughts:

_____
_____
_____
_____
_____
_____
_____
_____
_____
_____
_____
_____
_____

❦

Prayer Requests:

_____
_____
_____
_____
_____
_____
_____
_____
_____
_____
_____
_____
_____

❦

Prayers Answered:

_____
_____
_____
_____
_____
_____
_____
_____
_____
_____
_____
_____
_____

Precious in God's eyes

SCRIPTURE:

"She is more precious than rubies.
And all the things thou canst compare with her."

PROVERBS 3:15

ELUCIDATION:

Have you ever thought that you were no good because of your fears and your anxieties? Has Satan ever messed with you and told you lies such as "you don't measure up", "you aren't good enough", "you'll never do anything right", "you'll never be a good wife, daughter, girlfriend, friend, mother, grandmother, aunt"? He wants you to think negatively of yourself. He wants you to believe that you won't overcome obstacles in your life.

Instead of giving into Satan's lies, remember that you are precious in God's eyes. You are also very precious in your family's eyes. This verse even says that you are more precious than rubies or other jewels. Nothing can compare to the love that God feels for you.

REFLECTION:

The next time you start feeling bad about yourself, and your heart fills with uncertainty, remember what this verse tells you, that you are precious! Whenever you start thinking that you aren't good enough for a specific calling or task in your life, remember that you are more precious than rubies. Reminding yourself that you are precious in God's eyes and in the eyes of people that care about you. You are a good mother, aunt, grandma, daughter, girlfriend, wife.

PRAYER:

Lord please help me to remember how precious I am in your sight.
Help me to not beat myself up over the things that I struggle with.
Thank you that I am more precious than jewels in your eyes and
in my family's sight.

I'm grateful for:

_____
_____
_____
_____
_____
_____
_____
_____
_____
_____
_____
_____
_____

My Thoughts:

_____
_____
_____
_____
_____
_____
_____
_____
_____
_____
_____
_____
_____

Prayer Requests:

_____
_____
_____
_____
_____
_____
_____
_____
_____
_____
_____
_____
_____

Prayers Answered:

_____
_____
_____
_____
_____
_____
_____
_____
_____
_____
_____
_____
_____

Shield me. Protect me

SCRIPTURE:

"Ye that fears the Lord trusts in the Lord.
He is their help and their shield."

PSALM 115:11

ELUCIDATION:

When you fear the Lord, it doesn't mean that you are literally afraid of Him. Rather, fearing the Lord means that you know Him, and want to get to know Him. Whenever you are facing struggles in your life you can remind yourself through reading this verse that He will always get you through your struggles. when you trust the Lord and know Him personally, even though things might look and feel crazy in your life, trust that God is your help and your shield. He will shield you from the evil of this world and shield you from your anxiety.

All you have to do is ask Him to calm your thoughts and He will answer you. Maybe He will tell you to read His word or to lean on Him through prayer. Maybe He will tell you to go talk to a trusted friend and that friend will offer you encouragement. He will also shield you from bringing yourself down with negative self-talk.

REFLECTION:

Think about what God has shielded or protected you from. There may have
been things that He protected you from and you didn't even know it.
Thank Him for His holy protection over your life.

PRAYER:

Lord please protect me from my anxiety. Please protect me and
shield me from negative self-talk that can harm me. Please shield
my mind from Satan and help me to stay focused on you. Thank
you for shielding me from things that I may not even know about.

I'm grateful for:

My Thoughts:

Prayer Requests:

Prayers Answered:

Don't give into Anxious Thoughts

SCRIPTURE:

"Therefore, take no thought about the morrow for the morrow shall take thought of the thing of itself. Sufficient unto the day is the evil thereof."

MATHEW 6:34

ELUCIDATION:

This verse is important in your everyday life. It tells you not to worry about tomorrow for tomorrow will worry about itself. Think of the things that worry you and keep you up at night. Do you worry about what you will be able to accomplish the next day? How about worrying about your kids (if you have them)? Do you worry about your job? Don't keep yourself up all night worrying about things that will happen tomorrow. Try to only think about the tasks that you have to do today instead of worrying about tomorrow's tasks.

All worrying about tomorrow does is rob you of today's joy. Don't waste your energy worrying about things that haven't even happened yet. Enjoy each day as much as you can instead of worrying. Don't create fake scenarios in your head about what could happen either. Stay focused on each task in front of you each day and try not to worry.

REFLECTION:

What do you worry about? Remember that worrying takes away the joy you can feel in life. Don't waste time creating worse case scenarios that may not even happen. Instead, try to enjoy every day as much as you can.

PRAYER:

Lord please help me to not give into anxious thoughts about what could happen tomorrow. Please remind me that each day has enough troubles of its own and that you will get me through each day.

I'm grateful for:

_____
_____
_____
_____
_____
_____
_____
_____
_____
_____
_____
_____

My Thoughts:

_____
_____
_____
_____
_____
_____
_____
_____
_____
_____
_____
_____

Prayer Requests:

_____
_____
_____
_____
_____
_____
_____
_____
_____
_____
_____
_____
_____

Prayers Answered:

_____
_____
_____
_____
_____
_____
_____
_____
_____
_____
_____
_____
_____

Worrying is a waste of time

SCRIPTURE:

"Therefore, I say to you, do not worry about your life, what you will eat or what you will drink; nor about your body, what you will put on. Is not life more than food and the body more than clothing? Look at the birds of the air, for they neither sow nor reap nor gather into barns; yet your heavenly Father feeds them. Are you not of more value than they? Which of you by worrying can add one cubit to his stature?"

MATHEW 6:25-27

ELUCIDATION:

You don't have to worry about your life, even though this world will throw a lot at you. You might question where your next meal will come from, or wonder how you will make ends meet when money is tight. Whenever you start getting anxious remember what this verse says. If God can care for the birds, then you know He can and will always care for you.

Then it goes into asking whether you can add a single hour to your day by worrying. Sure, worrying might make you feel better in the short run, but it clouds your judgements about the future. If you worry, you will take your eyes off the blessings that are already in your life. If you only take away the time that you have by worrying, why do it? It will only disrupt your physical, emotional, spiritual and mental health. God wants you to trust that He will provide for you.

REFLECTION:

Have you ever felt better by worrying? You may feel better in the short term, but it takes your eyes off of God and cause you more harm in the long term. When you remind yourself that you can't add a single hour to your life, you won't waste time worrying. Trust that God will provide all that you need.

PRAYER:

Lord I know you will meet all my needs. Thank you for the point-blank reminder that worrying is not only a waste of time, but that it actually disrupts my physical, mental, spiritual and emotional health. Please help me to not waste my time worrying about life.

I'm grateful for:

My Thoughts:

Prayer Requests:

Prayers Answered:

Desires in life

SCRIPTURE:

"Delight thyself in the Lord and He shall give you the desires of thine heart."

PSALM 37:4

ELUCIDATION:

As a woman you have many desires. You want your life to go well. You want your kids to excel at school and in their careers and their marriage. You want you and your husband to have a good marriage. You also want to excel in your workplace and want your family life to be wholesome. Sometimes the pressures of this life can make you anxious and give you uncertainty about your future.

Instead of giving into that feeling, rest in God's promise that if you delight yourself in the Lord and make your desires known to Him by prayer, then He will give you the desires of your heart. Tell Him what is on your mind about your future, your kids, your marriage. You can talk to Him about anything and everything. Ask Him to let you know which areas that you need to work on in your life, with your kids and your marriage. Delight yourself by being in His presence, reading His word and getting closer to Him every day.

REFLECTION:

What desires do you have in your heart? Have you told God about them? Don't be afraid to talk to God about the dreams that you have. When you bring the desires of your heart before God, He hears you and will help you accomplish your dreams. He will move in mighty ways to make your life better than you can imagine.

PRAYER:

Lord please help me to know what areas of my life I need to bring to you through prayer. Help me to read your word and stay close to you. Thank you that your word says if I delight in you that you will give me the desires of my heart.

I'm grateful for:

My Thoughts:

Prayer Requests:

Prayers Answered:

Be Vigilant

SCRIPTURE:

"Be sober be vigilant, because your adversary the devil as a roaring lion walketh about seeking whom he may devour."

1 PETER 5: 8

ELUCIDATION:

This verse can strike fear into you very easily. You don't want to think that Satan is looking for you to devour you on earth. That is why it tells you in the verse to keep watch, to be vigilant and to be very aware of what Satan is trying to do so you can resist his schemes. He can attack at anytime and anywhere whether it is through an anxiety attack, or through an argument with your family, or falling out with a friend.

Those incidents can take you off course from God and into Satan's snares because Satan makes you think that it's ok to wallow in your anger and wallow in your own misery. Satan also makes you think that it's ok to not apologize to other people until you got an apology back from them. Rather than giving into the devil's schemes remain close to God. Ask Him to reveal the areas that Satan may be attacking you in your life. You can resist Satan's attacks by clinging to God's promises.

REFLECTION:

What areas have you noticed that Satan is attacking your life? Ask God to reveal where you are most attacked. Sometimes you may not even know what areas he is attacking. God will help you understand the areas where you are attacked and help you resist the devil.

PRAYER:

Lord please reveal to me where Satan is attacking me the most in my life. Help me to resist his attacks on me whether they be emotional, physical, mental or spiritual. Help me to stay close to you during my anxiety.

I'm grateful for:

My Thoughts:

Prayer Requests:

Prayers Answered:

Help me resist

SCRIPTURE:

*"The thief cometh not but for to steal and to kill and destroy.
I come that they may have life and that they may
have it more abundantly."*

JOHN 10:10

ELUCIDATION:

Satan can attack you and make you feel lonely, attacked and afraid, by reminding you that he only comes to steal, kill and destroy. But you can rejoice because God promises you that through Jesus, you will be given life and you will be able to live it more abundantly than you could ever hope for or imagine.

You can resist the devil when he tries to steal your peace and joy by saying testaments over your life such as: "I am a child of the most-high." "You will not be able to steal my peace or kill my joy because Jesus is in my heart and His peace sustains me." "You will not destroy everything that I've worked so hard for in my life because Gods hands are on my life and I will live it abundantly through His power." "You will not take away my abundant life. I will live abundantly through Christ."

REFLECTION:

What testimonies can you recite over your life when Satan tries to steal your pe and kill your joy? How do you keep your heart, soul and mind on Jesus when Satan tries to destroy your happiness? Remember that God will sustain you, even in the midst of your struggles. Give thanks to Him you can live life abundantly.

PRAYER:

Lord please protect me from Satan's attacks. Help me to be able to resist him. Help me to enjoy my life through your grace and mercy. Help me to stand firm on your promises that you will give me abundant life.

I'm grateful for:

My Thoughts:

Prayer Requests:

Prayers Answered:

Spiritual Dark forces

❧·❦
SCRIPTURE:

"For though we walk in the flesh we do not war according to the flesh. For the weapons of our warfare are not carnal but mighty in God for pulling down strongholds, casting down arguments and every high thing that exalts itself against the knowledge of God. Bringing every thought into captivity to the obedience of Christ."

2 CORINTHIANS 10: 3-5

❧·❦
ELUCIDATION:

Every day you're at war against the spiritual warfare of this world. But the good news is that even though you walk in the flesh you are not born of the flesh. You are a new creation in Christ. The weapons of war you face are not of this world but they are from God. He will cast down arguments within your family in His power. He will also bring down everything that exalts itself against Him in your life. You can bring your thoughts to obedience to Christ by keeping your mind steadfast on Him. You will be able to withstand the forces of darkness every day when your mind is on Him.

Try your best to think every thought about your life, the way God would think of it. You have mighty weapons of prayer, praise, and God's unconditional love to wage against the spiritual, emotional, mental, physical, and even the spiritual warfare.

❧·❦
REFLECTION:

What forces are against you in your life? Remember you're not of this world. Keep your mind on the forces of Heaven whenever you feel attacked by Satan emotionally, physically, mentally or spiritually. He gives you wonderful tools to withstand those different attacks such as prayer, worship, His Word and His love.

❧·❦
PRAYER:

Lord please help me to resist the physical and spiritual warfare that is against me every day. Thank you for having power over every force of darkness. Thank you for giving me the tools to withstand personal attacks by Satan.

I'm grateful for:

_____
_____
_____
_____
_____
_____
_____
_____
_____
_____
_____

My Thoughts:

_____
_____
_____
_____
_____
_____
_____
_____
_____
_____
_____

Prayer Requests:

_____
_____
_____
_____
_____
_____
_____
_____
_____
_____
_____
_____

Prayers Answered:

_____
_____
_____
_____
_____
_____
_____
_____
_____
_____
_____
_____

Comfort when lonely and abandoned

※·※

SCRIPTURE:

"A father to the fatherless, a defender of widows,
is God in his holy dwelling."

PSALM 68:5

※·※

ELUCIDATION:

Do you wish you had more family around you? Do you wish you had more friends in your life? Do you ever feel as though you're alone? God hears your thoughts and the sighs that you keep in your heart. He knows how much you long for people to be in your life. He knows who belongs in your life and who doesn't. Nothing that you think about is hidden from Him. God will bring the right friends and family members around you in His timing. Pray for the discernment to know who you should and shouldn't be around.

Have you lost your husband and are now a widow? Have you ever been abandoned by your father or family? That loneliness can feel overwhelming. God will help you overcome the feeling of loneliness and help you enjoy life. He is a father to the fatherless and He is a protector and defender to the widows. He sees your suffering and knows how you feel. He will put the right people in your life and He will protect you from being taken advantage of. He will bring people that will feel like family into your life. He will bring helpers into your life to help make daily tasks easier. If you've been abandoned by your earthly father, take comfort that you have a Heavenly Father watching over you at all times.

※·※

REFLECTION:

If you have ever been abandoned by your father or family, remember that your
Heavenly Father loves you. He wants what is best for you. If you're a widow, God
will bring special people into your life that feel like family. Isn't it comforting to know
that God is a father to the fatherless and a protector among the widows?

※·※

PRAYER:

Lord thank you for comforting me when I feel lonely or
abandoned. Please put the correct people in my life to remind me
that I can always ask them for help. Thank you for your protection
and for watching over me.

I'm grateful for:

_____
_____
_____
_____
_____
_____
_____
_____
_____
_____
_____
_____

My Thoughts:

_____
_____
_____
_____
_____
_____
_____
_____
_____
_____
_____
_____

Prayer Requests:

_____
_____
_____
_____
_____
_____
_____
_____
_____
_____
_____
_____
_____

Prayers Answered:

_____
_____
_____
_____
_____
_____
_____
_____
_____
_____
_____
_____
_____

Torments of Worry

SCRIPTURE:

"He shall cover thee with his feathers, and under his wings shalt thou trust: his truth shall be thy shield and buckler."

PSALM 91:4

ELUCIDATION:

Psalm 91 is all about dwelling in God's presence. It is all about resting in the shadow of the Almighty. Whenever you get weary from stress, anxiety or loneliness remember this verse that tells you that God will cover you with His feathers of peace. Let His peace cover you like a warm blanket as you rest in the promise of this scripture. You will feel His peace in your mind, soul and your body. You can trust in Him under His wings of safety. He will protect you from the lies of the enemy.

The truth of His word will be the promises that you can always stand on. The truth of His promises will be your shield against the Devil's schemes. Take courage that you can rest in the calmness and peace of God's presence. He will be your shield and reassurance in times of trials. Rest in His truth that you are His, that you have a purpose, and that He wants what is best for you. Find refuge for your soul under His wings. Rest in His promises for protection against the devil and the evil of this world.

REFLECTION:

This Bible passage can help you escape from the torments of worry. When you have time, read it in its entirety and you will feel a peace beyond your own understanding. A peace that can only come from God Himself. Rest in the shadow of the Most-High and dwell in the presence of the Almighty.

PRAYER:

Lord thank you that I can dwell in your presence any time I want to or need to. Thank you for filling my heart with hope through your scriptures. Thank you that I have your promises to lean on. Please protect my mind, soul, and body from the devil's attacks and help me to rest in the assurance of your love.

I'm grateful for:

My Thoughts:

Prayer Requests:

Prayers Answered:

Turn Worry to Worship

SCRIPTURE:

*"Why art thou cast down, O my soul? and why art thou
disquieted within me? hope thou in God: for I shall yet praise
him, who is the health of my countenance, and my God."*

PSALM 42:11

ELUCIDATION:

This scripture asks you questions directly: Why are you downcast? Why are you worried? Why are you so disturbed in your spirit, mentally, emotionally, and even physically? Then it invites you to examine and search your heart. It asks you to figure out why you are so on edge and upset. The best part about this verse is that it points out that you can put your hope in God. You can praise Him instead of giving into worry, anger, or despair about your life. You can turn your worry into praise and worship.

You can still praise God even in the midst of your struggles with stress, anxiety, fear and loneliness. When you take the time to praise God even in the midst of your circumstance it changes you point of view. It takes your mind off of worrying and puts your mind on worshiping the one who can and always will help you through your problems. Worshiping God will instantly make you feel better.

REFLECTION:

*Have you felt your mood change from dread, uncertainty and confliction to happiness
and peace when you go from worrying to worshiping and praising God? That is how
worship and praise can help you through any stress that you have. When you turn
your thoughts over to God, you can clear your mind and find ways out of
your difficult situations.*

PRAYER:

*Lord please help me to turn my worry into worship. Turn my dread
into peace through your power. Help me to still want to worship
you despite my circumstances. Thank you that you remind me that
I don't have to be so worried and upset about the way things are
going in my life. Fill me with your peace.*

I'm grateful for:

My Thoughts:

Prayer Requests:

Prayers Answered:

Free me from myself

※·※

SCRIPTURE:

*"The fear of man bringeth a snare:
but whoso putteth his trust in the Lord shall be safe."*

PROVERBS 29:25

※·※

ELUCIDATION:

You can easily fear what others can do to you, your family and your friends in life. The fear and stress that you have about your life can cause you serious mental, difficulties. You may not be able to think straight at work because you are constantly over thinking everything. It can cause you physical difficulties such as not being able to eat or sleep. You can't function without proper rest and nutrition. Insomnia can cause you to go days without sleep which isn't healthy. Stress can also cause you emotional difficulties such as sudden outbursts of anger, crying and fatigue.

Anxiety or loneliness can also take your eyes off God and bring you spiritual harm. Not being focused on God can make you think that you can get through difficulties without His help, and things will soon spiral out of control. The good news is, you are never too far gone from God's presence. You can always return to Him any time.

This verse reminds you that if you trust in the Lord you will be kept safe from physical, emotional, mental or spiritual harm. He is the one who has seen you through all of your other difficulties before. He will do it again. All you have to do is trust Him. He will free you from your anxiety, fear and loneliness.

※·※

REFLECTION:

Have you ever suffered sleepless nights and physical pain because of anxiety? Satan uses your stress and anxiety to make you think that you're fighting alone and that you have nowhere to turn. You have to remind yourself that you are kept safe by God from Satan's attacks. Speak God's promises over your life by saying: "You have no power over me Satan! I'm safe in God's arms. I won't let you shake me off of my firm foundation!"

※·※

PRAYER:

Lord thank you for freeing me from myself! Thank you for freeing me from feelings of loneliness. Help me to trust you every day.

I'm grateful for:

_____
_____
_____
_____
_____
_____
_____
_____
_____
_____
_____
_____
_____

My Thoughts:

_____
_____
_____
_____
_____
_____
_____
_____
_____
_____
_____
_____

Prayer Requests:

_____
_____
_____
_____
_____
_____
_____
_____
_____
_____
_____
_____

Prayers Answered:

_____
_____
_____
_____
_____
_____
_____
_____
_____
_____
_____
_____

Don't give up on Him

✦

SCRIPTURE:

"Being confident of this very thing that he who began a good work in you will compete it in the day of Christ Jesus."

PHILIPPIANS 1:4

✦

ELUCIDATION:

In this scripture, Paul and Timothy were telling the people of the church of Philippi that when things become difficult, Jesus who began His good work in their lives will continue working behind the scenes, in the background, in the middle, and even in the forefront of their lives. They reminded them that He would finish the good work in their lives.

His words are as true for you now as they were back then. He is working good things in your favor even when you can't feel or see yourself making progress towards where He wants you to be. Even when you think you can't go on, He has put a good work on your heart and will help you complete it minute by minute, hour by hour. Think about the dreams that God has placed on your heart and ask Him how He wants you to complete them in His name. Ask Him to give you the strength to complete the dreams that He has placed in your heart.

When you feel like giving up on what He has called you to do because you fear that no one will be interested, remember that's how Paul felt too. Remember that He put the dreams and desires in your heart and that He promises that He will help you bring the good work He started in you to completion until the day He calls you home.

✦

REFLECTION:

What dreams have you casted aside because of your anxiety? Has God reawakened them in your heart recently? Trust that God will help you bring the dreams to completion.

✦

PRAYER:

Lord please help me to not give up on the good works you have placed on my heart. Direct me in your paths for my life. Thank you that through you those good works will be brought to completion. Thank you that your hand is on my life with every step I take towards accomplishing my dreams.

I'm grateful for:

My Thoughts:

Prayer Requests:

Prayers Answered:

Not alone for God's with Me

❦·❧

SCRIPTURE:

*"See, I have engraved you on the palms of my hands;
your walls are ever before me."*

ISAIAH 49:16

❦·❧

ELUCIDATION:

Sometimes loneliness can be overwhelming in your life. If you don't have a husband, boyfriend or fiancé, and everyone around you has one, it can bother you. Seeing others have someone special in their life can make you think that you're missing out on something big. Have you ever blamed yourself and thought you weren't good enough for a man?

You can talk yourself into thinking that you might be alone forever. That's not true. God is with you and He has a good plan for your life. He has inscribed you on the palm of His hands. He knows who belongs in your life and when they will come into your life. Just because you may not have a boyfriend or husband doesn't mean that you're alone. You can do well in life even without a man at your side. If it is Gods will, you will be blessed with a man by your side eventually. Try not to rush that process. Let it happen naturally and with God's blessing over your life. You are engraved in the palm of God's hands.

❦·❧

REFLECTION:

Have you ever said that you were missing out on the dating experience? Have you ever blamed yourself for it? Have you ever thought that you wouldn't find a boyfriend? Take comfort in the fact that God will bless the person that you are meant to end up with if your union together is His will. Trust in Him that He knows what is best for you. Also remember that you can do very well by yourself. God also gave you the support system that you have around you with your family, friends.

❦·❧

PRAYER:

Lord thank you that if it's your will, I will have the correct person as a boyfriend and husband in my life. Thank you that you for the constant reminder that I am never alone. Please take away my loneliness and fill me with your joy as I wait for the right person to come into my life.